A Medley of Ruminations

Charmiene Maxwell-Batten

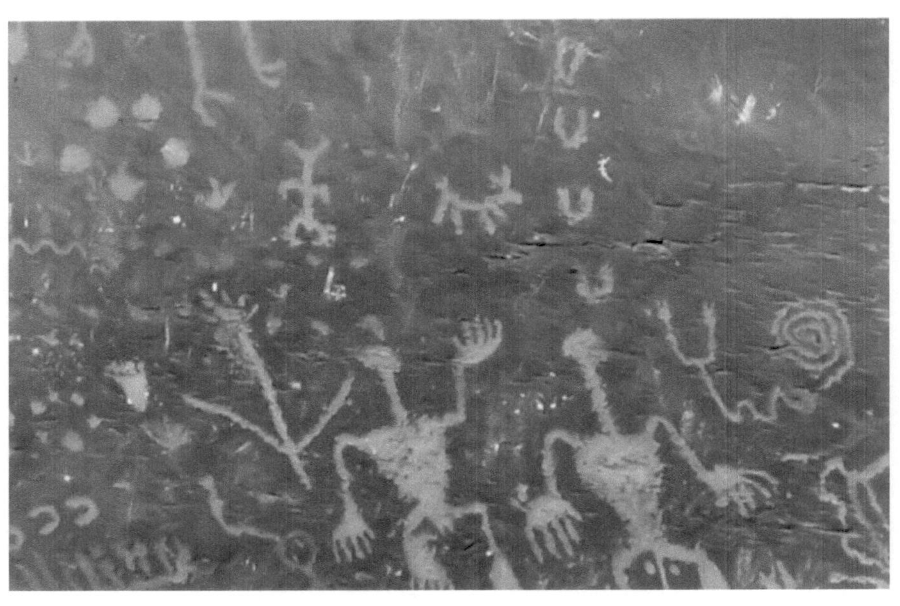

A Medley of Ruminations

Charmiene Maxwell-Batten

Copyright

ISBN 978-1-4710-2997-4

Second Edition

Printed in Europe

Contact:

charmiene_batten@hotmail.co.uk

http://www.lulu.com/content/10660744

Books

By Charmiene Maxwell-Batten

Araminta's Message – from the World of Fairies

A Journey in Thailand and India

England – The Song in my Soul

Switzerland – you Touched my Heart

Musings in America

Revelations of a Housekeeper

Childhood Reminiscences

A Life Lived

Murmurings from the Heart

Murmurings from the Heart Volume 2

CONTENTS

Acknowledgements

With profound acknowledgement to the philosophers, poets and authors who have through the ages and so courageously aired their own thoughts, reflections and emotions. Whatever era we might live in, most people hide innermost feelings. Those with a bold integrity, who dare to reveal subjective feelings, may be in danger of being misunderstood and even ostracized. It is with deep respect and admiration that I applaud those writers who have the guts to express their inimitable truth.

Sharing views openly and sometimes with enthusiastic naivety I live in hope that society can be enriched by a colorful array of each and every manifestation of uniqueness.

I salute with whole-hearted gratitude, all the writers who have inspired my journey through life. I devoured books by: Henry Miller, Gerald Durrell, Lawrence Durrell, Richard Bach, Stephen Levine, Charles Dickens, the intrepid Agatha Christie, Somerset Maugham, Ann Morrow Lindbergh, Emma Jung, Marie Louise von Franz, Elizabeth Kübler-Ross and more recently Michio Kaku and Prof. Brian Cox. . The works in Greek mythology such as 'Amor and Psyche', 'Orpheus and Eurydice' as well as legends and fairy tales from all over the world are an enchanting opportunity to study ancient symbols and language of consciousness throughout a challenging human journey.

Those books that have stirred a bright spark in many hearts' also have my deep appreciation; 'The Little Prince', 'Hello Mr. God this is Anna', 'Dibbs, in search of Self', 'Watership Down', 'Jonathan

Livingstone Seagull', 'The Way of the Peaceful Warrior' and so very many more.

Thankyou.

Dedication

To my parents

"Only love can be divided endlessly and still not be diminished"

Anne Morrow Lindbergh

Mum and Dad's grave in Topsham. I bought the statue of the otters for Dad because he loved otters and wildlife. I bought the other statue of mother and child for mum. Their grave is unique here.

Mum and Dad in East Africa in the 1950's

Sadly, dad lost the bulk of his photos in a fire during the late 1970's while living in Topsham, and many of his remaining photos were damaged.

Introduction

"Let your Soul be your pilot"
Sting

Immersed in writing, I feel soothed and take a breath of deep relief like anyone who is impassioned and stirred with inspiration. Without analyzing where others may find that place of relief, there are people who can hardly wait to run off and have a cigarette or a coffee, which may be a comparable sensation. I rush off to my lap top computer and write. After having spent timeless moments of personal expression in what I call writing meditation, I'm profoundly aware of our interwoven, collective and connected web of cosmic existence.

There were more stories to write after previous books were seemingly finished, so this book was named '*A Medley of Reflections*'. Many of these reflective stories delve into our human psyche; the inner universe of shared humanity is worthy of exploration and certainly arouses my curiosity. I've no desire to ostentatiously churn out self-help recipes into an already overly saturated market, but instead to question, seek, consider and ruminate. Being a little jaded with the 'New Age' era of books that come pouring forth offering numerous techniques, opinions and even dogma to an apparently starving arena, I distance myself from the boisterous seers and visionaries who may appear frantic to market a new-fangled vision to those searching for answers. Many people seek ways to better cope with hectic lifestyles.

Childhood issues and torn emotions are purported to be diagnosed and remedied in many fashionably motivating books, while showcasing brightly smiling and magically enlightened faces of authors. I find myself neither seeking nor offering guidelines or techniques, but simply inviting the reader to join me on this journey of looking in. Self-help jargon can certainly be a helpful condiment where a supportive or healing environment may seem absent in our lives.

'*Having a short daily nap will prevent heart attacks*', were the words jumping out from a health magazine that was filled with pictures of vibrant people bounding around with glittering smiles. Of course it's wonderful advice, yet the majority of hard working individuals are expected to work robotically and not permitted a short afternoon nap.

The modern age of numerous advice-giving authors are able to make money on the coat-tails of big corporations who are creating the problem in the first place; corporations whose treatment of employees has never been seen as health orientated. Promptings in self-help publications often serve to remind people of what they don't have time to do. It can also become a sticky and addictive trap where there is no end to the methods or techniques to reach happiness. I know of countless and ever hopeful individuals who after twenty years, are still on the treadmill of paying for workshops, therapy, groups and motivational literature to improve the quality of life. Copious therapists, psychics, healers may presume to know the right recipe for their clients to overcome suffering and their enthusiasm is visibly genuine.

The diverse and vulnerably mortal reflections in this book expose our human journey with thoughts, feelings, and even questions. if I were to point towards a possible direction, it would be to hope and pray that compassion and wisdom will spread throughout our society and that each person may add to that goal by becoming genuinely aware not only of themselves, but of the world around us - that's all.

At Zurich Airport.
Charmiene in her twenties –
'Reflecting on life'

The End of the Rainbow

With a dreamy lightness in their eyes I've heard people say 'there's a pot of gold at the end of a rainbow'. Is this an illusion or a fantasy to deflect from difficult realities?

Is it a longing for the relief of peace? Is it a lively desire to achieve goals or is it simply put, the base instinct of greed which drives people to own those 'riches' - a pot of gold that may exist somewhere in the distance?. Is this allegorical pot of gold a hoax and illusion or a metaphor for the hope that keeps us searching for nirvana?

Like Northern lights sweeping across the Arctic skies in soft pastel or vibrantly striking colors born of the union between earth's magnetic field and a solar flare, a rainbow is just as breathtaking and always beautiful. The caressing rainbow colors are lavishly available for our eyes to feast on and our soul to drink. To be the exclusive owner of this radiance on a physical level is impossible, yet it is entrancingly captured in poetry, paintings and in music. It can't be owned. Though many seek this pot of gold, coveting and even attempting to grab it with whatever means available - it nevertheless remains unreachable. To some, it's a burning passion to achieve noble goals in their life.

A paradox! The pot of gold is ours. The rainbow is ours. It's given freely and lovingly for us to see and feel in our heart. It can't be sequestered in a personal bank account. It can't be hidden away in a box far from the view of others and attempting to do so this will encourage greed and more misery. This shared rainbow is accessible to all of humanity and belongs to no-one. A Zen koan and a riddle. Perhaps a time will come when humankind appreciates the rainbow is an inclusive gift. Maybe then we will actually see and find that mysterious pot of gold.

My mother made me laugh when she went through her 'jumble sale' phase, rushing off to the local jumble sales with her basket, ready to grab and even snatch items of clothing away from other grasping hands. She had such humor, and did it with a bouncy and mischievous spirit, almost caricaturing that trait in people who saw the act of grasping as a serious project. Or perhaps she really was grabbing what she could. When times were hard and our mum realized that being polite and gracious didn't seem to work very well in the milieu of jumble sales, she launched into a renewed gusto by joining in the rough and tumble scene while rummaging through the stalls of second hand items. She wasn't a bit afraid, in fact it seemed more like an adventure to her. She was pleased with all her purchases, telling us how another person had tried to grab things from her and she held on for dear life.

Mum wasn't always the playful spirit, but when that quality was expressed in her, she shone a lively light on many things and it was uplifting. I think she found that pot of gold.

"The Final understanding is that -
Love is all there is"

Ramesh Balsekar

The Flower Girl

They called me the flower girl.

Walking through fields, along streams and rivers, an abundance of sweet wild flowers welcomed anyone who walked those paths. Fused with an individual color and fragrance while imagining that each flower had a story to tell, my unplanned walks were mostly alone but not lonely because I was engrossed in picking wild daffodils, primroses, violets, daisies and anything I could find to make a pretty bunch of flowers.

After handing a cluster of flowers to the elderly neighbors in Woodmead road where we lived in Lyme Regis, I went home feeling really happy; a sense of joy was magnified when seeing the pleasure it gave to people who spontaneously received a handpicked bouquet from the hands of a child.

I've always loved flowers. They've not only been loyal and treasured 'friends, but they seem to have an uplifting effect on everyone. I still remember that Christmas day at our lovely home in Dorset, 'Woodlands', when I unpacked a box filled with petite and colorful plastic pieces, which when put together in the right way became big beautiful flowers. It kept me happily fascinated for hours. My parents instinctively understood this affinity to the floral world. Even as a young girl living in Africa, Dad bought me a spray of sweet smelling carnations for my seventh birthday. Skipping off to my bedroom so as to gaze at the pink frilled petals and breathe in the aromatic scent of blossoms as often as I could before they faded away became irresistible. Carnations had a fragrance in those days. How amazing that my father knew what an idyllic gift that was.

Like many children, I had a scrapbook where dried flowers were pasted onto each page with names and descriptions; going on a nature walk to collect an assortment of plants became an exciting and intriguing adventure. Later in life, being absorbed in the study of medicinal herbs, my nightly reading was focused on the fascinating literature about remedial components of plant life and botanic medicine. I still feel quite upset to see people destroying what they presume is a weed, when it often has healing properties.

I'm in love with herbs, flowers and trees. Our home in Texas became a garden of joy where I spent hours being totally absorbed in planting, digging, nurturing and watching our garden grow. I find it therapeutic, loving and rewarding and I'm not sure I could ever live without flowers.

"Lo, the winter is past,
The flowers appear on the earth"

Song of Solomon

The Banana Tree

A positive visualization of sitting under a big banana tree gave me a sense of peace whenever time to unwind was vital.

Sitting under a big leafy tree, feeling relaxed and unthreatened by schedules and timetables gives one a chance to gather thoughts and reflect a little, before marching forward into everyday elemental activities.

The feeling of having some timeless moments was important at different times in life especially when the energy for outward expression wasn't easily accessible. Often making a pot of tea, sitting quietly and drinking from a delicate china cup symbolized a time to go inside and touch base with an inner core of my heart. Re-charging inner batteries can give one a feeling of composure and renewed strength.

When sunbathing on the sandy beaches of Hawaii, a hat that resembled an exotic lampshade conveniently covered my face so that I felt shrouded in a haven and a hideaway. My hat transformed the milieu of a crowded beach into a protected sanctuary. Two of my friends had the same thought when they purchased an identical hat.

After living in Alaska and discovering an unexpected source of strength in the environment, I found that talking, connecting, laughing and being amongst people in a natural way regenerated a very real enjoyment in being an outgoing person. With this enhanced vitality I didn't need the protective banana tree anymore – I thought!

Alas, when my laptop computer was stolen ten years later, it occurred to me that this was my banana tree where I felt soothingly secluded within a bubble of writing. The original symbolic vision of a banana tree was at that time a way to hide, whereas the laptop was a way to connect, yet both enabled a welcome retreat into a meditative cocoon.

Friends sometimes believed that I was being distant when immersing myself in a cocoon of peace, yet I had to laugh when at other times some people displayed signs of envy when a cheerfully gregarious 'me' emerged. Mingling and enjoying life in a more outgoing way was and is still a part of me. People tend to judge and make shallow assumptions often based on projections.

I've now learnt to honor whatever encourages genuine, personal happiness and peace no matter what conjectures are made. My stance is to be sincere, whether quietly retreating into a sanctuary or vivaciously dancing amongst friends. I've not been interested in simulated or spiritual retreats or a pretense at being sociable and bubbly because I need life to be authentic. I laugh from my heart when happy. When silently alone I'm not lonely.

The banana tree was a symbolic friend. Finding places and symbols of rest may mean that we really can slow down, and reflect a little on the life we are living.

I still value my banana tree to this day.

Sunset on the Estuary in Topsham

The Energy Game

Can we manifest a meeting of our higher selves in the hope of resolving base relationship issues that occur on the heavier level of human filters? I first became aware of this idea while living in a communal house on Dartmoor in England. The shrouded moors of Dartmoor are known for their vortex of energy and enchanting ambience of mystery.

That night while sound asleep, it was as though I were meeting Sophie and Dave without the burden and shackles of a physical form or human emotions or even mortal judgments. It was a light hearted gathering filled with the clarity of lucid understanding. Their etheric essence seemed to be whooshing around visiting people in a playful way, without the restrictions of gravity.

It seemed that I was being shown what one can do with the lightness of energy. Since that time and over the following years I've heard a lot of new-age spiritual jargon about the higher self and astral travel, which are indeed fitting descriptions for this otherworldly phenomenon. It allows for non-verbal communication that may possibly heal and resolve existing issues on the 'ground level'.

On the baser human echelon, I was uneasy with the way Sophie and Dave had set themselves up as guru and assistant. The 'lowly' spiritual seekers, who came to see the couple, were expected to surrender to Sophie's rules and doctrines. The openly egotistic, harsh and even cruel treatment of the numerous spiritual seekers who had gathered around this pair concerned me, and knowing it was a trend at that time for spiritual teachers to be hard hearted, I wasn't willing to accept that without question. In fact, my encounter with Sophie and Dave turned out to be quite dramatic in the end.

Sophie had explained to us that as a baby she was aware of a choice, whether to cry in her cot knowing that she would be dependent on someone meeting her needs, or wait quietly without any desire for overt attention. She chose the latter and at that moment she became enlightened – as her story goes. That story impressed me and many others. Was it true though? She went on to explain that growing up at school had been difficult because she could see through the masks people were wearing and she didn't always like the real person behind the mask. Hence, she was considered a strange and odd youngster among her peers. She was teased and ridiculed at school and her worried mother took her to an assortment of therapists.

According to Sophie and her devoted followers, ordinary people didn't understand her unique state of spiritual enlightenment. That too was impressive.

The eight of us, who lived in the house, were considered fortunate to be so close to the 'enlightened one'. Every week, the household would leave the picturesque dwelling and go to the small historic village of Totnes where spiritual seekers gathered to hear Sophie's sidekick, Dave, give a lecture, answer questions and monologue about the 'truth of life' while Sophie sat in silence, in her apparent enlightened state. Sophie was a strange girl who at twenty-three years old was physically very beautiful and not afraid to exhibit her sensuality to the males around her. She seemed to be playing the role of the seductress and the oppressor. She reminded me of the cruel and scheming queen in fairy tales. Though I inwardly questioned her sanity, I couldn't explain the fact that so many ordinary and intelligent people seemed simultaneously intimidated and in awe of her. Is this a signal of a con artist with charisma and skill?

At the house, some dedicated and curious students of the spiritual path would come to visit on a Sunday. They were hungry for knowledge and eager to find the meaning of life. Their efforts and enthusiasm were met with denigrating comments from the oracle Sophie. After witnessing her rude, cruel and belittling treatment of these trusting students, I decided I would candidly question her method of teaching. She seemed to be exploiting the power that was so unquestioningly and gullibly handed to her.

The fact that I even doubted Sophie's approach instigated a deluge of deriding comments and attempts to browbeat me into submission. Suddenly filled with a quiet yet astonishing strength within my spirit and not in any self- doubt, I stood firmly by my truth. Knowing that I needed to expose a malicious cult in the cleanest way possible before more people got hurt – I did. In some instinctual way, I knew that my actions had to be one hundred percent pure and without any emotional baggage in order for me to rise above the scheming Sophie. During the theatrical events that followed, the commune fell apart after the police arrived and the two leaders went scampering back to Bristol. In all the years since that episode, I never once doubted the clear and conscious action I took.

I was convinced that Sophie may have had a glimpse of spiritual enlightenment but lacked the maturity and compassion to be a healer or a teacher of wisdom. She seemed to be abusing power and indulging in a self-serving desire to control 'her followers'; anyone who questioned her was met with a team of bullies. Sophie and Dave's teaching did not come from a place of love, but a place of iniquity and narcissistic dominance.

I left with gratitude because of having found the strength to confront a seemingly powerful, manipulative and even devious game of power. I was also very glad to have experienced and understood the 'dance of energy', which was a positive occurrence in this communal setting.

Now many years later, I wonder if Sophie and Dave are teaching with perceptive maturity, and less ego.

Soon after leaving this episode behind us, Scott and I went to India and quite coincidentally met the eighty-three year old sage Poonjaji; I knew that a real enlightened being who had depth and compassion was present, yes, he could also be harsh, yet it was not cruel because his message was filled with love.

It's clear that there are spiritual teachers or leaders of cults and even some mainstream religions, who will lead people astray. It's a precarious path where the best and most trustworthy directions come from the core of your own heart.

Divinity is found inside and not outside.

Let us listen.

"This soul now reads what the clouds write
on the face of heaven,
And what the breeze draws
on the surface of the water"

Kahlil Gibran

Stealing

We'd been gone for just ten minutes when they broke into our car. Kali, our dog, was quietly hiding under the front seat; she seemed bewildered as her brown eyes blinked with a questioning expression. Our first response was '*Thank God she's safe*'. We'd just arrived back in San Antonio after being in Arizona for a week and our prime thought was on groceries for our evening meal.

This theft occurred at a time when we were facing a variety of hurdles and I was still in shock at the recent death of my father.

My laptop, as well as LeRoy's vital and meticulously assembled seminar notes, were stolen. Our new camera with some irreplaceable photos of Stonehenge - also gone.

For the last three years my friend, the lap top computer, had been a lifeline, akin to a comfortable pair of slippers where I could lose myself in a world of writing. My coping mechanism was snatched away within a few minutes.

For the people who steal, it must be a 'high' of some kind; its quick money for sure. There can be no comprehensible awareness in the mind of the stealer as to the wave of hardship that a theft instigates in a person's life. My own loss was trivial when compared to some situations, nevertheless, I spent days having to protect my record of identity by placing fraud alerts on personal information which had been stored on the laptop. Stealers would need to anaesthetize themselves emotionally in order to ignore and even hide from the awful consequences of their actions.

The police thought that some jobless youngsters had broken into our car on that early evening. Others thought that it could be the wave of homeless people from New Orleans, who had lost everything themselves through the tragic floods, and were now trying to pick up the pieces of their own lives.

I can't even imagine the grief caused to anyone whose home and sanctuary has been broken into. The pain and heartache caused when a pet or child has been kidnapped must be unbearable. The abuse and rape of children is a tragic theft of their innocence with terrible life-long repercussions and consequences.

I felt extremely vulnerable for weeks after the shock of realizing that someone had invaded a 'safe' place, which turned out to be vulnerable.

The calculating action of wealthy people who pay their staff as little as possible is an obscure and just as culpable form of theft. Corporations who shell out huge and decadent salaries to top executives and yet deprive ordinary hard working individuals of a decent standard of living by skimming as much as possible from their remuneration, is also robbery.

Is thievery carried out by humans against one another a sad yet harsh reality of our society? Is it just for survival? Is it envy?

How do we cope with loss? Passive resignation or anger and frustration at injustice? I suppose my way, which seems to release any resentment or righteous anger, is to remember the words of a spiritual teacher in India '*Whatever we can lose was never ours anyway; what is real, can never be lost'*.

Six weeks later, still going through the ache of losing my father who unexpectedly died during that time and the loss of my friend the lap top, was a tough experience because to me, it was more than a mere computer. To the thieves, it was an object.

"BE A ROSE WHO GIVES FRAGRANCE
EVEN TO THOSE WHO CRUSH IT"

Kahlil Gibran

Berries

Reddish orange berries spread in a big clustering mass on the sidewalk became a symbol of support on that afternoon. Those colors brought relief in a moment of aching emptiness.

Whenever I began a new assignment as a home caregiver away from my own familiar surroundings, an unstoppable gasp of loneliness mixed with the sense of being utterly lost overwhelmed me each and every time. Those feelings don't have words; it's an unexplainable ache.

As I walked down the road towards the shops on that first day, with the familiar sensation engulfing me, I knew there was no escape except to ride it out, then I saw the bright red berries. Stopping and gazing in a timeless moment, I was breathing in the life-giving colors because they gave me hope and in that instant, they were a lifeline.

It's impossible to define an emotion with which to identify that powerful sensation; one can only 'be it' for as long as it takes. Having also experienced this sense of timelessness at the most beautiful and exquisite scenes, I wasn't afraid of allowing 'the gasp' to be there; it is a moment of pure sensitivity flooding through one's body and soul. I have no choice but to feel it.

While living in Alaska, each time I drove down the steep hill to my apartment in bootlegger's cove in the city of Anchorage, I was mesmerized by the dramatic beauty of an icy panorama in front of me; all I could do was to gasp in awe – therefore I know this state of 'gasping'. I know not to fight it. There's a painful type of gasp and then there's another gasp where one is touched by the divinity of nature. I believe that dancers, singers and musicians know that gasp, which carries you into a realm outside the restrains of a logical and of a learned constrictive mindset. It is so total; one has no other choice than to yield. I believe it's the river of life for want of a better comparison, and I'm willing to flow with the river. What other choice do we have?

My two-week assignments as a caregiver in England were sometimes tough when an elderly person living in their own home resented the intrusion of anyone. At other occasional times an elderly person was welcoming.

Nature itself was and still is a constant and much needed comfort in my life.

Cosmetics and Clothes

Wearing make-up and choosing clothes has a multi-faceted significance. I've heard someone talk about power dressing when she wanted to summon the courage to confront a difficult situation. Others shop for clothes and cosmetics, so as to alleviate a feeling of despair. Whether a permanent addiction or a temporary boost - clothes, make-up and shopping may certainly have an uplifting effect. Buying that new lipstick has fortified many women; it's given me a boost of cheer on a few occasions.

My friends, Alice and Amalin are primarily responsible for introducing me to the joys of wearing make-up, earrings and cheery clothes, not to impress nor to disguise the real person, but very simply to feel happy and extend that feeling of joie de vivre to others with the added expression of clothes.

I was just about fifteen years old when I met my dear friend Alice Dunham after my family moved to Marshwood, in Dorset. Even though the fashionable era of skinny Twiggy was being unleashed into our impressionable young minds, I was nevertheless a skinny unattractive teenager whereas Alice represented the epitome of glamour. Her bedroom became a boudoir for creating new hairstyles and trying out the latest make-up. I found myself welcomed into the latest and enchanting world of femininity and fashion. I bought some inexpensive pink earrings when we went shopping on one occasion. Fifty years later, just the memory of my pretty pink, wooden earrings still brings a splash of cheerful thoughts to me. Those earrings seemed to transform my feeling about myself because I felt pretty for the first time. On another lipstick-exploring shopping trip with Alice, I purchased a trendy lipstick, which made me feel modish and eye-catching. Even in those days, it wasn't a superficial investment in adorning the body; it was the youthful and playful delight in using colors, cosmetics and decorations that has stayed with me throughout my life.

A few years later, while living in Hawaii during my early thirties I met my friend Amalin Grooms, who was often seen as flamboyant, dazzling and outgoing. Before she found herself on the New Age path of spiritual seekers, she had been a highly successful Image Consultant in Boston USA; her impeccable taste in clothes and make-up was not pretentious, excessive or inauthentic, indeed she glowed with a sense of sincere elation through her mode of dressing. When our paths crossed again in Lucknow, India, while visiting a spiritual sage, the same lively manifestation of color and cheer reflected in her clothes and make-up. She drew me into this world of vivacious expression, which again wasn't a mere façade or a veneer to cover and disguise the 'real person' - this was the real person!

Since those times, I've always felt that same sense of energy and enjoyment when decorating my body with color, beauty and elegance. Amalin showed me how to dress gorgeously without it being costly, and it was all achieved with a wonderful sense of adventure that didn't require stress or tension. A happy endeavor!

Some people nicknamed Amalin '*The Duchess*' and it wasn't always meant kindly. Perhaps they were envious and unable to understand the vitality she exuded, but I'm glad she was free of any need to tone down her exuberance. Amalin was highly accomplished in finding inexpensive clothes that were captivating and striking.

Ever since that time, when I'm in high spirits and filled with vitality, it reflects in the clothes I wear and the make-up that I adorn my face with. It's a visibly heartwarming way to be in harmony with our body.

I'm aware that many people wear make-up to cover an emotion or as a symbolic barrier between their inner world and an outer expression of personality, which is sometimes necessary in unfriendly surroundings. Another aspect was expressed very touchingly by someone recently, who said that even though she may feel devastated by personal challenges, wearing make-up gave her a sense self-respect and strength to cope with the harsh ordeals in her life. Yes, it was a veneer that she fully acknowledged, but a conscious facade that motivated courage and dignity.

Like everything in life, clothes and make-up can be a playful and uplifting source of energy and a way to deal with and confront challenges, although if it becomes an addiction and creates dependency, tension, stress and rivalry rear their ugly head and submerge the spark of fun and enjoyment.

I'm so glad I experienced and learnt the joys of adorning my body, from two good friends and beautiful souls.

"Life Stands before me
Like an eternal Spring
With new and brilliant clothes"

Carl Friedrich Gauss

Crutches

There are symbolic crutches where people instinctively discover ways to motivate themselves throughout a lifetime. Breaking or injuring one's leg calls for a physical crutch, which clearly allows mobility and support during the healing process, until the prop isn't needed anymore. Emotional crutches are not always so obvious, even though they may be just as essential for encouragement and healing.

Thrust into the chaos of human existence, there are times when the need to find an anchor or a helping hand is elemental. A temporary disability is being coped with by a provisional fortification – the crutch. It can be a subtle transition or a conscious step into a path of dependence when that crutch becomes an unintentional and permanent fixture.

This is especially visible with the wretched snare and addiction to painkillers or any other way of easing the ongoing discomfort that a number of people have found themselves caught up in.

Vital factors that have enriched and supported me personally are writing, dancing and gardening. Walking into a room and seeing my lap top computer has triggered an immediate and elevated sense of welcoming that seems to pervade my body and my spirit. I've even found myself acknowledging the little silver 'life form' with the warm playful words: 'hello lap top. That same friendly feeling cheered me as I walked into my flower filled apartment in Alaska. My friend Chinmayo first alerted me to this delightful greeting, when with an expression brimming with joy she told me how her flowers welcomed her home as she walked through the door.

On days off from work I could barely wait to immerse myself in our garden in Texas; gardening revives, soothes and comforts me. Just walking around the garden and greeting the flora gives me great joy as I visit each and every plant. I can never resist waving to the colorful hibiscus from our kitchen window.

Maybe alcohol or cigarettes provide an essential escape and reassurance to some people - how can one reproach that need to find comfort? A crutch is at best, a temporary and not a permanent support.

I'm not sure that 'a crutch' is really an apt word for the things that help us cope and survive an often harsh world, because it implies being disabled. We all feel like a bird with a broken wing at times; the comfort of music, flowers, exercise, writing and perhaps even cigarettes helps to heal the injured wing.

Is a crutch a way to escape from oneself? No, surely not, unless we become addicted to it. A spiritual sage once described addictions as clandestine habits that are hidden in shadows, as he urged his students not to smoke in guilt-ridden secrecy but to do it in the light of conscious awareness.

Music brings with it numerous memories of events linked to a specific era and it's easy to bathe in warm recollections brought on by the sound of a familiar tune; the music from the movie Gladiator always inspires me with renewed strength and the belief in my own resolve. I think it also reveals the endurance and stamina to survive hardship. When the most recent music touches our human soul, it brings with it a fresh stream of inspiration. There is something about music that helps one touch base with one's soul and unite with the divinity of life. The memories of music from my 'Osho days' feels like soft falling rain bathing me in a comforting recognition that there is more than this bodily life.

If I could formulate a difference between the symbolic connotation of crutches and a figurative banana tree that gives a sanctuary of respite, I would say that the one helps us when we are incapacitated and the other is a way to stay healthy and vibrant by recharging our human batteries.

Dào

I'll Find My Way Home

The song by Jon and Vangelis, 'I'll find my way home', had a profound effect and was embraced as a source of emotive release by a milieu of spiritually orientated friends during the 1980's. It evoked, in me too, an elevating message.

Living in Switzerland at the time, I'd just embarked on a path of Eastern philosophy and the so called 'search for truth, nirvana and enlightenment'. For many young spiritual seekers, this song set free the tears of a divine longing for their inner home.

Throughout our mortal pathway we do experience moments of feeling lost and music frequently offers a tender hand of solace. All those years ago when I heard that song by Jon and Vangelis, there arose a sensitive awareness that whatever and wherever 'home' is - it can be felt. Now when hearing the song, I'm bathed in sweet memories of a melodious time where 'finding my way home' had the sentimental and arousing effect of feeling it close to my heart.

The river seeks the ocean and can't stop until it reaches its destination – can we stop? It is the journey home.

What is home? It has occasionally been portrayed as a form of escape to an imaginary idyllic and far off planet where delusional and crooked leaders of certain cults have made it a seeming reality by cashing in on that deep seated and collective pining for sanctuary. I think home is something inside oneself. Home is a deep acceptance of oneself – of being truly at peace in the 'here and now' without giving in to the enticing ruse of a temporary illusion.

"The ache for home lives in all of us.
The safe place where we can go as we are,
And not be questioned"

Maya Angelou

“Madam”

In America it’s ‘Ma’am’; I’ve never been comfortable being addressed by either of those seemingly formal modes of salutation because I feel that it creates a chilly boundary between people. Though I’ve been told in Texas that it’s considered a polite form of addressing someone, it nevertheless does often denote an immediate aloofness and even separation.

In England the term ’madam’ is cloaked with a variety of connotations. A shop assistant may use it to stroke the ego of puffed up ladies who enjoy being venerated; on the other hand, I’ve heard hotel reception front desk agents using it in a very down to earth and warmly sincere greeting towards their guests.

An undertone of this pigeonholing, which recently exasperated me, occurred when I objected to a discrepancy that arose in a well-known and up-market food store in England. The young shop assistant switched to a rigidly cold voice, her posture tightened as she called me ‘madam’, while evading the problem. Turning triumphantly to her colleague, she gave the impression that she was proud to have had a dig at someone she considered to be a member of the well-heeled establishment. I imagined that she had a chip on her shoulder with an ensuing crusade to defy the prosperous echelon of society. I saw the farcical humor in these oversimplified assumptions.

I don't have a regional accent. From my speech and bearing alone, I could be mistaken for someone from the prosperous ranks. Money and/or accent can be a ticket to include or exclude anyone from the pre-defined stratums existing in England. There's a mixed bag of people who have a non-regional accent but don't have money and therefore, form a new-fangled group who find themselves in a limbo of the 'social order'. In the past a noticeably refined accent was linked with money – not so anymore. I heard someone say: *"we're a new breed, floundering around to find our niche in society"*. She went on to say: *"I don't seem to belong in either the prosperous echelon or the grassroots of society that has been established through regional accents"*. I thought she had a point!

When someone feels motivated to call me 'madam' because of my accent or to emphasize an exclusion from the milieu of regional accents, I do get a little ruffled; from my perspective I'm at ease in each and every rank of social grouping. My criterion lies in the human element.

I'm surprised that a word can still be used to prolong and accentuate a long-established barrier between social groups.

"*Every leaf speaks bliss to me,*
Fluttering from the autumn tree"

Emily Bronte

"The most
massive characters
are seared with scars"
Kahlil Gibran

Abandonment

We've all felt some form of abandonment - by another person or simply said, by life itself. Other times we may carry an unnecessary burden of responsibility or conversely the justified sense of culpability for having deserted someone in his or her time of need. It's in moments of distress and aloneness or low times of grief and isolation that the human spirit usually needs the support of others.

Feeling abandoned or abandoning another person brings an array of emotions. I've known men and women who feel cast off when a loved one leaves them or a longtime friend deserts them, particularly at a time of vulnerability. It's not personal and there can be no blame metered out; one can only say in honesty, that one feels alone.

Being unexpectedly in need of help is often and sadly mistaken for ever-present 'neediness'. The value of warmth, friendship and encouragement can't be underestimated. As individuals in society, we've created impenetrable capsules for ourselves; rallying around others in times of suffering often seems a bother. Turning one's back on someone because of a hidden fear of the effect it will have on us personally is a denial of our own humanness. Do we cover up an inability to face wholeness with a sparkly and shallow show of denunciation and when that heavy cloud hangs bleakly over others, are we reminded of our own desolate and well-hidden place of gloom?

I heard someone quote that in an instant of mortal vulnerability when Jesus was on the cross, he cried out in pain: *Father why have you forsaken me'*? Feeling abandoned in a fleeting moment he allowed humanness to be expressed. So why do we need to hide from our own humanness?

I was impressed when hearing the story of Marie Louise von Franz (one of my favorite authors) who went to her cabin in the mountains equipped with cross country skis; she wanted to spend some time confronting everything and anything that arose from her inner world of thoughts and feelings. Loneliness, fear and even abandonment are all emotions that can create havoc in the daily lives of many, yet people will often evade and hide from an inner world that is filled with the kaleidoscope of human emotions. Marie Louise Von Franz wanted to shine a daringly candid light into the hidden corners of her psyche by consciously removing outside diversions; her objective was to face each and every thought that arose. After suddenly realizing with laughter and recognition that skiing was also a way to be diverted from intense emotions that are conveniently veiled by the commotion of daily life, she summoned the courage to remain in this cabin alone and face herself – and she did.

There are participants in some progressive therapy and meditation groups who sit willingly in silence for hours, while watching the thoughts, feelings and even physical discomfort that arises. The lure of impulsive reaction is diminished by this conscious witnessing of thoughts. Thoughts are like clouds; when we cling to a negative thought pattern it is as though we are engulfed by a cloud of confusion and the clarity of vision has been wiped out. By allowing the clouds to float by, gives rise to a sense of acceptance, tranquility and alertness.

Every emotion is an inevitable part of our mortal embodiment, nevertheless I'm sure the human mind will always try to find reason, logic and even blame for those emotions. I felt that I had abandoned my young brother as a five-year old little boy when I went to Switzerland and left him in England, in difficult circumstances. I felt responsible because he needed stability at that time, yet I was a girl in my twenties without much strength of character and compelled to work and earn a living. I feel that I abandoned my beautiful sheltie dog 'Passion' when I left her in San Diego with a loving family so that I could go on a long trip to India and Thailand. How easy it is to carry guilt on our shoulders instead of compassion for one's own actions.

Attributable to childhood trauma, abandonment issues may inopportunely pop up in adult life as a knee jerk reaction, especially when those past scars have been buried with the elusive notion they will evaporate; therefore the feeling of abandonment can be a recurring and painful predicament like a 'tape recording' that is being played over and over again. The value of watching those past-related emotions and facing them with pure honesty is profoundly and blessedly liberating.

Misunderstood

When we have a perception of ourselves and others see us differently, do we feel indignant? Do we submit and become overtly passive yet inwardly rebellious, just to appease? Haven't we all felt misunderstood and hurt by those 'fast food' assumptions made by others? On the other hand, there are those rare observations made by others that do ring a bell of truth. If there seems even a grain of validity from another person's observation, then it's worth reflecting on.

With all the years of oblivious indoctrination and brainwashing instilled since childhood, our human mindset does form opinions. A cultural and collective behavioral pattern automatically ignites an agenda of labeling. The brain itself, a brilliant bio-computer, will organize the massive amount of incoming information by using past input to make sense of any newly received information. Is it then surprising that assumptions can be made? No amount of judgments or categorization made by others need be taken personally.

I do object to the numerous therapists, psychics and so called "gurus" who do occasionally force self-righteous opinions on others. In a pitiful determination to prove themselves right, they may systematically obliterate any words arising from their 'prey'. The value of listening on all levels has been superseded by a display of persuasive authority and dominance. Whoever can shout the loudest seems to gain supremacy in the eyes of gullible students. I have attempted to query certain shifty advisers, guides and spurious mediums - only to find that the level of defensiveness, knows no bounds. Those gullible students may often feel overwhelmingly misunderstood in this scenario.

I wonder why people generally fall short of resolving a notion about someone else in a more direct and a fair-minded approach instead of making intriguing guesses. Is it too simple to just find out in a guileless way? Or has the thrill of scandal and gossip made the colorful field of conjecture much too enticing to renounce?

When you have fire in your soul it takes a certain character to recognize and soar with shared joy – as dancers, actors, writers and artists can do. To be faced with a lifeless and bland expression can be frustrating when one feels impassioned by life. In my own moments of elated animation or a heartrending aching of the soul, I admit to feeling misunderstood by anyone who seems to remain motionless, emotionless with an expression of wishy-washy colorlessness, or an attempt of any kind of robotic, uninvited advice.

Paradoxically, dolphins in their intrinsically non-verbal, non-judgmental empathy, will feel your pain and your joy; they will 'dance' with you. Is it so difficult for humans to learn that?

"When you feel the suffering
Of every living thing
In your own heart,
That is consciousness"

Bhagavad Gita

Diana and Pavarotti

She died in 1997. He died ten years later.

Princess Diana and Pavarotti both had totally giving spirits – he to music and she to humanity. They brought a breath of love to the world.

Watching the media pictures of this charismatic pair walking together on that sun filled day, I was touched by the glowing spark of unity in their shining presence. Colorful and vibrant, both were overflowing with life and love.

He brought an infectious laughter, joy, passion and aliveness to opera and to the world. She was not afraid to share her unique spirit of beauty, compassion and humanity. What a loss to the world; yet these bright lights will continue to touch the spirit of humanity with the hand of divinity, for eons to come.

Lynn

Lynn's melodious presence was evident to anyone who came her way; a caring friend who hears, shares and listens. While trying to cope with a sinking feeling of despair, Lynn's cheery and sisterly welcome ignited a sense of hope and buoyancy in my drooping spirit. An immediate camaraderie with this bighearted human being, resulted from a chance meeting.

Caring for the elderly took me to different parts of England on a two-week rota; I was leaving an assignment when Lynn was beginning her two-week rota. Her yellow and orange beachy clothes were like sunshine that day, not the harsh midday sun but the comforting warmth of midmorning, when one feels relaxed. That first impression was to be ongoing. I had met a new friend whose inherent personality was kind and thoughtful. Little did I know on that July day how much the unswerving encouragement that this empathetic friend gave to people would mean to me, just five months later.

There existed an inherent and much needed support system with most of my fellow caregivers; we were a concerned and compassionate team where there didn't seem much help anywhere else. One is thrust into some unbearable situations and great comfort is found in talking with other caregivers who understood the spectrum of trials and ordeals that are presented in this occupation.

I went to visit my friend Lynn in Fowey, Cornwall where she lived; it was an enchanting area where two days were filled with friendship, honesty and laughter. Coincidentally, Lynn was taking care of her mother's Jack Russell dog, who was a cuddly, lively ball of affection and joy – I love dogs. A ferryboat took us on a fun trip to an intriguing Cornish village for a pub lunch; Daphne du Maurier's house and the bookshop that was filled with her memorabilia, was enthralling. I took numerous photos and felt a familiar yet almost forgotten sense of playfulness return to my soul.

The difficulties and challenges that Lynn had been forced to confront during her life and the strength she found to move forward, touched me deeply. This unexpected sanctuary allowed me to expose the overwhelming wave of sadness I still felt after the recent death of my father and the ongoing trials that my sister presented. A grey dark cloud was lifted from me that day as I proceeded with a lighter and grateful heart. After those two days of soothing, cheerful and heartfelt chatter, I knew that angels are around.

THE SHIP INN
The Ship Inn
LOCAL FISH
DAILY SPECIALS

Non-Entity

Do you feel regarded as a non-entity sometimes? It may very well be that someone is behaving towards you with that in mind.

Domestic staff can typically be seen as non-entities by employers who delude themselves into thinking they are paying for a service without the 'nuisance' of any human connection. Yet how do we as a collective humanity deny anyone's basic entitlement to expressing a personality? Of course it's reasonable to curb a predisposition towards dysfunctional, wacky or anti-social tendencies – nevertheless, why deny the elemental and enriching quality of anyone's authentic personality?

On occasions, I've felt robotically spoken to in establishments such as banks, shops and even a library. Particularly in this age of telephone call-centers, the human element is conveniently erased so as to obliterate any last trace of empathy. It seems paradoxical that American hotels place an inordinate amount of emphasis on techniques that highlight and train the staff to demonstrate empathy towards their guests

– in fact empathy, has by default become a buzzword. When working as a hotel receptionist in Texas, I naively took it for granted that empathy is a natural outcome of being authentically concerned for the well-being of others. Surprisingly, those in-depth training programs with the accompanying jargon didn't have any effect except to produce a lot of spuriously talking and smiling robots. Is it possible that a number of hotel staff are covertly bitter towards their guests when behind the painted smile lurks a thinly veiled resentment? The effort invested in smiling artificially, clearly results in surreptitious antipathy. I'm not sure that I even have a better idea for 'training techniques' in order to create skills in the area of empathy, but for my own part, an honest pleasure in the rapport and association with hotel guests added to the enjoyment of my job, which in itself produces an inherent friendliness and requires no excessive struggle or need to feign responsiveness.

Then there is that blatant unconcealed lack of responsiveness at the checkout stand of some supermarkets, big shops and stores. I take umbrage when a checkout cashier prattles to a friend while keying in my purchases, only speaking transiently to me as a shopper just to conclude the transaction. The customer becomes a necessary nuisance who is interrupting a gossip session. I came across this behavior in Texas. Perhaps some of those Texan youngsters in thinking themselves 'cool', motivated a disinterested scowl towards 'outsiders'; 'outsiders' being the customer.

When strangers acknowledge you with a smile or briefly, unpretentiously make eye contact, one can't help but feel a sense of wellbeing. When those who work in shops, banks, libraries and hotels smile and see you as a person, it warms your heart and it warms the world we live in. It is vital for people to be seen as sentient beings, otherwise a controlling yet invisible boundary becomes non-productive and even antagonistic.

Do humans treat each other as non-entities in order to avoid involvement; is it a way to feel superior or just a basic lack of interest?

I speak to everyone in the same way,
whether he is the garbage man
or the president of the university."
Albert Einstein

*"The opposite of love is not hate.
It is indifference"*

Christopher Pike

*"Desire is half of life,
indifference is half of death"*

Kahlil Gibran

*"Love cannot endure indifference.
It needs to be wanted.
Like a lamp, it needs to be fed
out of the oil of another's heart"*

Henry Ward Beecher

The Wobbly Man

He was light blue colored except for a conical shaped red hat. His cheery smile and expressive face were inexplicably heartening to me.

At that time I was attending St. Michaels School in Lyme Regis on the Dorset Coast, it was just one of numerous schools before the age of ten. I still remember that comforting wobbly toy sitting on my desk and smiling at me; we were allowed to bring a familiar and reassuring item from home into our arts and crafts class at school. Most kids brought their Cindy doll or a teddy bear or even a small and treasured ornament. The teacher wanted her pupils to feel comfortable in the class. It was certainly a relaxed and welcoming environment.

From the moment mum bought me this unusual toy, he represented a cheery protector and gave me the feeling that it's okay to shiver, shudder and wobble in life and still smile like he did. The ability to gently bounce up again no matter how often one is pushed down was very meaningful to me during those vulnerable years. I am amazed at my mother's perceptiveness, to have given me something that brought so much comfort and epitomized such meaning. I think she also took an immediate liking to this sweet toy and couldn't resist bringing him home. The wobbly man symbolized my young journey in life at the time, where we don't need to take things personally; we can allow ourselves to wobble and yes, we can smile through the storms of life.

I wonder what happened to my intriguing wobbly friend because I don't remember seeing him once I started Grammar school at the age of eleven; though after a recent conversation with my sister I was reminded that he had been broken and I discovered that the broken concrete, which lay at the base of the wobbling mechanism was an anchor. Did I too lose my anchor? I wonder who broke my wobbly friend....was it my sister who then tried to patch him up again. My younger sister, in her childlike hope to repair the damage, brought a Band-Aid to patch him up. I look back with love at those sporadic memories of my sister's kindness, because in our later years she seemed to have developed narcissistic tendencies where she saw me as a villain; her caustic jealousy of me became obsessive as she saw me as competitor instead of sister.

I am saddened by this.

Two for Joy

I saw two magpies crossing the road while I was driving along a coastal path in North Devon; one of them was hobbling painfully across the hard tarmac, possibly with a broken leg or wing. I was astounded to see the able-bodied magpie walking slowly beside the injured bird and even though a car was approaching, he didn't abandon his weakened friend. It really touched me and tears of emotion were welling up as I witnessed compassion and loyalty in the bird world. Maybe they were a couple, like swans who stay together. Risking being run over by a fast moving car so as to protect a friend was truly humbling to watch.

At that moment, I thought about the well-known traditional folk tale about magpies:

'One for sorrow, Two for joy,

Three for a girl and Four for a boy.

I'd seen only one magpie during different times in my life and although I don't take omens too solemnly nor am I overly superstitious, I nevertheless couldn't help feeling a twinge of disappointment whenever I saw only one of these long-established birds of prophecy and I had only seen one for so many years.

Seeing two magpies crossing the road right in front of me, gave me a feeling of hope that day. I immediately thought about my sister and how we seem to hobble through life trying to 'cross roads'. Outwardly, I'm always helping her across those symbolic roads, because she seems to have a 'broken wing'; yet, in that moment I was aware that there are other levels of unseen dimensions where she may help me to cross those allegorical roads. Maybe it's me who has the broken wing!

I had mostly only seen one magpie for so many years, which meant sorrow according to the legend, so I was thrilled to see two, even if one of them was hobbling.

'I'll take two for joy,

The Garden of Peace

A tranquil spot set amongst flowers, trees and rivers – a gentle place where the heart can be open.

A 'bridge' or the start of a journey to paradise? Or maybe it's a garden where the soul lingers for a short time before moving into the next world?

Resting on the soft grass, sitting amongst flowers that never die, being shaded by green leafy trees and bathing in clear blue water – love and friendship everywhere. Of course it's a fantasy that I'm sure we all share yet far removed from the often-harsh reality of our worldly life.

I wonder why extreme religions often frighten people about the afterlife with threats of 'burning in hell' if you don't surrender to their rules. What rules? I can't see it that way, I see an afterlife of consciousness that is connected to love and wisdom and this has become my own individual vision of the next step, after the death of our body. It's a vision that led me to writing about the possibility of a futuristic and more expansive outlook on our human 'dying' process.

The era of hospitals is undergoing some scrutiny and the means of departing our mortal life within the walls of a clinical environment is not an inviting prospect. Even the hushed up epidemic of the 'superbug' is enough to put one off even going into a hospital. As an alternative choice, I imagine a beautiful garden created especially for those who are ready to embark on a journey to the next world. A garden where one chooses to feel at peace, loved, happy, content – indeed to feel in your element. I would prefer to face the inevitable in a beautiful setting, than to fight it within the walls of a hospital – where people often struggle to escape the inescapable. I want to depart with dignity, consciousness and love - when it is my time.

I once saw a science fiction movie where in the year 2070, overpopulation of people and of course the greed of the privileged echelon led to the annihilation of trees, rivers, fields, flowers - nature itself had been exterminated. There were no trees or flowers anymore. As a result, a politically based system had evolved where poor people of a certain age were compelled to end their life; there were no exceptions to this man-made law – except for those who had wealth and power!

Accompanied by their younger loved ones – in this fictional glimpse into our future, the older person was given a lethal injection while watching a film about the beauty of nature, which didn't exist in any other form except as a film. It was a sad representation of mankind's future linked to the self-serving nature of the rich and powerful leaders who throughout centuries have never learnt to 'love thy neighbor'.

This is not what I had in mind with my vision because I am hoping for a higher level of awareness and wisdom for our shared future; I am hoping for a future where power and wealth become a little less enticing to mankind. A future where humanity could evolve with love in mind, instead of greed. A future where human beings will make consciously altruistic choices.

The garden of peace I envisioned is a futuristic place where we may spend our last days and hours surrounded by real beauty, real nature, real flowers, real trees and real trust.

"Let yourself be drawn
by the stronger pull
of that which you truly love"
Rumi

Seeing Isn't Believing –

Believing Is Seeing

The power of mind over matter has been an aspect of much discussion and debate. Most people have heard about a prayer circle and the power of prayer, where miraculous results have occurred. A potent and blessed vortex of concentrated and invisible strength that emerges from the heartfelt depths of our soul can't be measured scientifically at this moment in time. As science progresses and our brain evolves, the vision of energy that influences matter, which for centuries has been known to heal individuals in the face of despair and in spite of an inevitably gloomy prognosis, will be made visible.

Can we risk allowing the ego, which is filled with the mind's shallow desires, to corrupt the integrity of pure hope? I don't believe that a focal point of energy based on a craving for a bigger house or more money will manifest in the same way as the heartfelt core of energy that is focused on healing. We have a lot to learn from dolphins in their remarkably altruistic form of 'desire', which is so far removed from the egocentric cravings that most humans are burdened with. Beyond the mind there is an energy vortex created by the heart and is born of love – this is the effectual flow that can create miracles; yet it must remain innocent and free from the shackles of human egotism. The pragmatic outcome of positive visualization, even for prosperity, riches or for a bigger house has been encountered many times, yet it is of the essence to realize that a happy and liberated mindset as opposed to a grasping approach is the authentic way to trust in the purity of those aspirations. Positive thinking and happy thoughts do render healthy and robust body cells – that's been scientifically proven! A needy and tense mindset deprives body cells of vital oxygen. The body and mind are so closely linked!

With purity of the heart, deeper layers of vision are possible. Believing is seeing.

I'm a Reader

Not a Fortune Teller!

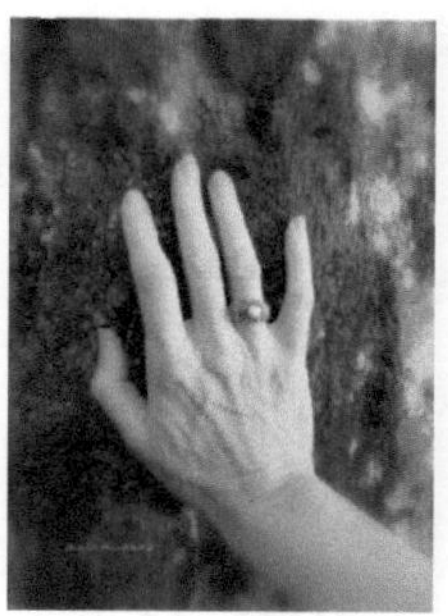

There exists today, in various cultures and even some bygone ways of thinking, a fixed idea that fortune-tellers, psychics and intuitive readers can work magic so as to conveniently manipulate destiny. In a desperate attempt to force the object of their love or lust to reciprocate with matching adoration, people may run off to the nearest soothsayer in desperation. Another myth is that the personified oracle can supernaturally enable a person to win money or lift a self-made and illusionary curse!

Are people looking for magic tricks?

Of course we mortals need hope. We seek ways in which life can be happier and more positive – not too many of us are interested in looking a little deeper into ourselves because a quick fix has become fashionably undemanding.

Psychics and fortune-tellers have been known to exploit this need for the manifestation of a dream. Sometimes a pipe dream is made to seem a realistic goal by materialistic soothsayers who entice vulnerable people to fork out money for the delivery of their goal, which could be a flight of fantasy. I've seen some psychics and readers often trying to convince even themselves that they can see into your future.

Having applied myself as an intuitive reader for a number of years, I sense that with quiet humility one can reach out to the heart of another person. The symbolic images in the tarot cards are helpful in guiding and navigating a pathway towards individual and collective harmony, which creates a better future. I've never been comfortable with a banal fast food culture of imagining one can wave a wand so that all desires will be fulfilled; to delude anyone by that promise of gratification can be wounding. We can surely focus thoughts in a selfless way thereby maintaining a relaxed and cheerful sense of potential for the manifestation of an aspiration. Ultimately it's a matter of Grace and not human intervention that determines whether this longing will be fulfilled. Sadly, most mortal yearnings stem from an egotistic craving and not a loving heart.

While living in Hawaii I was immersed in a lighthearted milieu of people experimenting with the trendy concept of positive visualization. What stood out for me was a playful and heartwarming wish to manifest love, prosperity, fulfillment, career and fertility without clinging to a needy craving for the fulfillment of this manifestation. A spirit of freedom and respect for the bigger picture was evident.

When my grandmother returned to England from Mexico City with her daughter (my mother) she settled in St John's Wood in London before moving to Devon. While in London, her son was killed in a motorbike accident at age sixteen, after which my grandmother frantically frequented psychics, mediums, séances and spiritual churches hoping to contact her dead son. It became an obsession and like an alcoholic, she began to feel dependent on the enticing words of clairvoyants who charged a great deal of money. Fortunately, they moved back to Devon after the doctors' warned my grandmother that she would lose her daughter too, who was being neglected and became very ill. The green and therapeutic countryside in Devon proved to be a healing time for them both. My mother's affinity to the simplicity of nature deepened her own highly tuned and natural intuition.

There are various levels and dimensions of 'seeing'. I'm in no doubt that some individuals authentically exemplify an ability to 'see' and intuit while picking up on deeper levels of 'language' or codes that may not be accessible to most people. I don't doubt the power of remote viewing or clairvoyance – and I absolutely respect indigenous cultures whose religious and healing foundation is based on a time-honored concept of the supernatural.

Modern day individuals who truly embody that gift are usually very low key. I've known two people who almost died and came back with what one calls 'the gift', yet they didn't feel any need to advertise or even sell it. They were not compelled to convince anyone that they are psychic. One of these people worked in a supermarket as a cashier – that's all she wanted to 'do' and through this she was able to help others in an inconspicuous way. Conversely I've come across people in several countries who, in an attempt to sell their wares and convince the 'buyer', some overly contrived words sounded more like a sales pitch. As though to dominate and crush any doubts in her audience one lady exclaimed: *"I'm a priestess!"*

Apparently, she needed to emphasize a perceived identity, which exemplifies the desire for self-importance. With the same evident need to convince me and with a matching inflection of authority in her voice, another lady insisted that she speaks to dead people.

There are shady individuals who attempt to frighten and cajole people into believing that a curse has been placed on them and, as anticipated, it would cost a substantial amount of money to 'lift the curse'. A pitiable and even gullible demand for 'magic tricks' will unearth countless willing volunteers to supply this demand.

Do we really need to see into our future? What compels people to mistrust the mystery of life? Do we imagine that it's our individual future when in truth it's a shared hope - a 'painting' that involves a myriad colors. Wouldn't it be boring to know exactly how our life will unfold and are we so afraid of that mystery? Conversely, there exists a deeply disturbing and fanatical code of belief that condemns any glimpse or preview of the future; individuals who see it as a sin and affront to their religious belief, unleash this castigating doctrine. Both attitudes seem disparaging because I can well imagine that the original biblical words are spoken with wisdom and compassion, not with fury; they were to guide people gently so as to release any craving to know their future.

I believe we can tap into our own intuitive ability; we can all come to terms with the 'here and now' without relinquishing hope; we mortals can also try accepting the reality of a sometimes painful world and thereby find peace. That is real magic!

"It might just be Love
that holds the stars in the firmament
and imposes rhythm on the ocean tides..."

- Maya Angelou, 1928 - 2014

Letting Go

How do people forgive or let go and even release the hurt or pain that they feel? Pain that is seemingly caused by another person, especially when it's been a parent or sibling, is hard to release.

While listening to a friend who felt the heaving pain stir in her chest and abdomen, I was acutely aware of her sadness as she spoke to me: *"It's hidden – it doesn't speak in words*" she said *"I want to let go, I'm tired of hiding from this pain; I want to feel light, and I don't want to bury this sorrow anymore".*

I felt the ache of her recollections. The impact of those memories and feelings that Amelia had been carrying for so many years were a consequence of the fear and violence she had seen during her childhood and teenage years, which had left her with a vulnerable wound. She related the details of her father's outbursts, and though the hurt was tough to bear, she nonetheless had the wisdom and consciousness to understand that her father could not control his temper; his behavior stemmed from an undiagnosed and hidden psychological dysfunction due to a wretched childhood and the horrific years of World War Two.

She just wanted to release that burden now; she had no desire or energy for vengeance, nor did she carry hatred - she wasn't 'in denial' either. Amelia only wanted to let go of the heavy weight in her chest.

When her father became an old man and lay in a hospital bed with very little time to live, she knew that he loved her because he told her so. She was suddenly and inexplicably able to let go of the past hurt; she realized that letting go is something you can't 'do' and you can't force – it simply happens at a moment in time that may not even be in our control.

The last time I spoke to Amelia she was at peace; the pain had gone and with a deeply inherent compassion, she understood the struggles that each human being is challenged with. Compassion gives birth to forgiveness. Forgiveness is born of Grace. True understanding of each other liberates the blossoms of love.

Stirring the Mud

When mud lies at the bottom of a clear pool of water or a pond, it solidifies and is hidden; the water has the façade of appearing clear, restful and beautiful. Try stirring the mud and the whole pond becomes murky. After some time the sludgy mass will settle at the bottom and nobody would ever know it was there unless they stirred it up or had the vision to see through the clear water, through the depths and all the way to the bottom. On a scientific level this mud is teaming with micro biotic life and contains valuable nutrients for the future of plant and animal life.

Metaphorically speaking, stirring mud and then allowing the fresh movement of running water can wash away the permanently stuck mass thereby allowing the water to be truly clear - all the way to the bottom of the pool.

Once the mud is recognized and allowed to wash away there is tremendous gratitude towards life itself. Idealistically, a person may try 'stirring the pool' within family or personal friendships, using a long and perhaps too determined stick thereby creating murky and disturbed waters. The person stirring the pool may often be written off as a troublemaker. Knowing there was mud at the bottom, this 'advocate for truth' stirred the pool - nobly wishing to 'clean' it up in the hope of instigating honest interactions.

Noble intentions can be misunderstood if they are not presented in a tactful or sensitive way. An enthusiastic and optimistic intent when presented bluntly is seen as disrespectful and even rude. Furthermore, it's futile to stir a pond where there exists resistance or a need to cling to this hidden mud.

It is possible to stir the waters and through this action discover the deepest beauty instead of mud, which instigates great healing. Interacting with people who are committed to consciousness and willing to wake up is gratifying; those who wish to hold onto the mud by defending and even justifying it, certainly have a right to that prerogative. It is a choice. There's timing for everything. Stirring the mud too quickly may in some cases cause serious and intense dysfunction in some people.

During my younger years I was continually stirring things up in the hope of revealing absolute honesty; stepping on anthills and being stung by angry ants was often the consequence. The desire to speedily get all the mud settled again by those hostile 'ants' was desperately obvious and even felt safe to those who held onto it: *'Everything back to 'normal again - don't allow the mud to be seen and DON'T stir it up - that way nobody need look at it; we can pretend it doesn't even exist'.*

Feeling sadly frustrated by that stance, my determination to stir it all up became as passionate as another person's desire to hold onto the mud. My yearning to communicate with the core of each human being was ardent; I didn't wish to talk to what I saw as mud filled barriers.

Alas, I had to let go of my passionate desire for frankness and ultimately in my own letting go there arose the shattering of a painful illusion. By suddenly realizing that I too was holding on to a concept and in my arrogance, I had even seen my task as significant. I was now embracing a far deeper wisdom.

Attempting to reach others in an authentic way can be approached softly and lovingly. When someone holds tightly and desperately to falsehood, this is their entitlement and their choice and may even be their only means of self-esteem at that moment. Why waste energy in trying to break down a steel door – why not allow others the space to guard themselves if they need to. Why not move to the doors that are open and welcoming! I was also holding onto a falsehood myself in thinking that I could simply and inconsiderately break down barriers.

While deeply understanding the space for each individual's need to protect that secret place within themselves and by seeing my own desire to connect on the deepest level with another person an invasive probing may have been prompted.

There arose a new humility – 'who am I anyway to 'want' something from another human being'; if it should happen naturally then let it be so. I now know that acknowledging each individual's choice is a loving and harmonious way to live life. Letting go is beneficial and the only path with which to express respect towards others and to one self. I am tired of stepping on anthills.

The Native Americans say that you cannot know what another human being is feeling unless you have walked in their shoes.

This allegorical narrative was first written ten years ago when absolute truth was vital to me, I just couldn't cope with people telling bare faced lies and now I've found compassion in knowing that people deviate from truth for many reasons, fear or a need to impress, being some of them .

"Muddy water is best cleared by leaving it alone"

Alan Watts

Now I am older and hopefully more aware, I can see the wisdom of this quote.

"Love is the only mirror we must use to judge ourselves and others."

Bodie Thoen

"Muddy water,
let stand,
becomes clear"

Lao Tzu

All the Lonely People

"All the lonely people where do they all come from?
All the lonely people - Where do they all belong"?

Paul McCartney and John Lennon

Advertising for grievers to attend the funeral of an elderly lady who had recently died and had lived her remaining days in a nursing home, this sadly unusual announcement in the newspaper caught my eye. At such a momentous time – the end of her human journey, it was disquieting to discover that this eighty-two year old lady had died, lonely and without anyone to express a final and loving farewell. Yet she had a life, a long life, she was once young and according to the article, was a dancer filled with vitality. This forsaken lady had no children – is that the sad criteria for someone to grieve for you when you're 'gone'?

Without children and grandchildren, our family becomes 'horizontal', comprising friendships, which turn out to be valuable and vital. With the growing pyramid of future generations, the flourishing family becomes comfortingly 'vertical'.

A further newspaper article shocked me to the core as I read about a quiet young man who had been found dead in his apartment. Nobody noticed how he was suffering and nobody knew his depth of desolation. He died alone and friendless. A struggling student from Africa, who could barely afford to eat, he had not succeeded in gaining financial assistance to enter University, in England. He hadn't known where to turn for help.

Watching a television documentary about people who die alone and unseen, it's clear that there are varied reasons why some people can't ask for help – their voice may not be heard or they may feel a dreaded sense of failure. Too embarrassed to reach out for support, their silent cry is left unheard. There are others who have no compunction in demanding financial and government assistance, even for bogus or self-serving reasons. I continue to hold hope for evolvement into a higher level of awareness as long as the unfairness of our human predicament continues to be imbalanced.

Countless people are lonely. Children, grandchildren, friends, family and pets alleviate that loneliness, while they are around. A number of people of various ages will join communes, religions, cults and even gangs just to feel that sense of mutual camaraderie. Reaching out for a community of sharing and caring so as to find a common thread of identity with others provides a feeling of unity and even a sense of being part of a family.

Regrettably, there are those who malevolently manipulate and take advantage of that need for kinship by establishing a group and hierarchy where they position themselves as 'the leader' of a cult, religion or gang. It's a tricky snare for the vulnerable, needy and lonely seekers of love and friendship.

While out and about with my camera, I saw an elderly man lying on the beach whose brown motorized buggy was parked at the top of the steps. A pang of melancholy swept over me as I imagined how he must have struggled to physically maneuver himself down those stone steps and on to the pebbly beach below, so as to lie in the sun's comforting benevolence for a while. A walking stick by his side was evidently the only support in his effort. I'm sure he was relieved to warm his aching bones on that day, after a damp and cold winter season. Lying in that contorted position, he didn't look comfortable and I wondered whether this elderly man was lonely, did he have anyone to help him? He looked lonesome. A consoling thought for me was that the pebbles he lay on were warm and soothing.

The widening gap between the affluent elderly who have appeared pampered as well as more than adequately cared for, and the modestly humble sector of our ageing society who struggle valiantly through the challenges of physical decline, concerns me greatly. I personally prefer to take care of elderly people who have very little monetary resources; their appreciative and lovable nature has touched me deeply on many occasions. The often materialistic and prosperous elderly have given me good reason to become apprehensive and even critical, because alas, I've seen a selfish and tyrannical quality to numerous well-heeled and ageing members of English society. I profoundly hope that someday, the fortunate sector of our community could possibly demonstrate compassion in their heart, so as to alleviate the despair of their less prosperous peers. I continue to hope for miracles!

Mum's Runner Beans

Mum eagerly lead me outside the small, low-income dwelling where she was living at the time; we clambered down some stone steps and out to the small plot of earth that had been allocated to her. With the excitement of a child, she proudly pointed to a row of green flourishing runner beans, which she had planted and cultivated from seeds. The runner beans were producing a vigorous harvest - I hadn't known at that time the extent of dedicated commitment required to grow those succulent green beans. Years later, my sister explained how mum had spent hours digging and preparing the ground; Mum chipped away at the barren parched soil where clay, gravel and debris had compacted together. Mum was not admitting defeat as the sweat poured down her back during hot summer days and the arid earth was lovingly transformed. Mum gave her heart to this small back garden and even cleared some space for a small square of grass to sit on – it was her way of transforming a bleak setting into a 'Garden of Eden'; she could sit on her small square of grass and feel in touch with the sky and the distant fields. She grew artichokes and tomatoes too! The elderly man in the flat below had never heard of artichokes and he called them 'anchovies'. He kept saying to Mum: "Nobody has ever grown anything there before". My sister recently explained how mum had dug the numerous stones from the ground and put them all in a sack, together they dragged the sack over to the edge of a field and emptied the grit and stones out. She carried bags and bags of top soil from the shops, all the way home and out into the developing garden.

I was twenty-nine years old and couldn't yet fully identify with the driving force of optimism that compelled Mum to breathe life into this tiny piece of neglected land. Now, as a more mature and weather beaten individual, the same compelling impulse to find courage, to create beauty and to radiate optimism in the face of challenge and adversity leaps into my own life. I too find it wholly uplifting to produce a flourishing garden.

While living in Alaska during harsh winter months and eagerly awaiting the summer weekend yard sales, I sought out limp, struggling and wilting flora in order to revive, renew and nurture them back to strength. My apartment became filled with healthy, green plant life, which ultimately revealed a sense of purpose and renewal. I felt a bond with my plants.

As related to me by my sister, Mum had been through a tough time when an arsonist burnt down the house where she lived with my sister and young brother, in Topsham. After being re-located to a low-income area that was particularly unsettling, she made the best out of a difficult situation and coped with feelings of desolation by growing a garden. By touching the soul of the earth, she was embracing hope in her heart. By giving love, tenderness, tears and courage to the earth, the bright spark of hope and warmth was given back to her, from the earth. I understand that now because like my mother, I can't renounce hope, I can't yield to a mistrust in life. I too have found that the healing action of gardening, writing and photography has not only inspired an awareness and a need to create beauty, but it's also imparted renewed hope; I cling to that sustenance. Without wishing to deny the existence of 'dark clouds' in our life's journey, I'm determined not to be engulfed by them. Not many understood how mum fought to survive the heavy clouds of our collective and human challenges; she refused to succumb to the numbness that most people have yielded to. Yes – many have forfeited that intrinsic gift to respond with sensitivity to the capricious tide of our life's journey. Many never recognized that brightly courageous cry of hope, even assuming that it came easily to my mother.

Mum's tireless bond with cheeriness was filled with action – it was alive and motivational. I've met people who express a limply feeble and self-orientated echo of hope without any determination or strength to back it up; I've seen people exhibit an oppressive verbalization, a thud of hope locked in the past with a weighty lack of enthusiasm to manifest action.

Mum's demonstration of hope was packed with action, and courage. In my late fifties, I was profoundly aware of this need to express hope in the form of action; it gives me a reason to breathe.

Mum's runner beans are a symbol of optimism, a deepening love and a willingness to feel.

Floating

I saw a hawk floating above me.

This bird had an absorbing effect, suspended in the air, unmoving and silent. Feeling impelled to stand still and watch the hovering hawk, I fell silent.

Convinced that numerous new age devotees would have copious opinions, suggestions and guidance in an attempt to find reason and meaning in this happening - for me it was a simple yet propitious encounter, which I acknowledged with gratitude; though I would undoubtedly listen to the conscious unembellished message from a true-blooded Native American, if offered. Mostly, the invariable prattle flowing vociferously from contemporary self-made Shamans, seers and channellers often seems like hollow noise.

For a few weeks prior to my trip to San Francisco, I'd been rushing around trying to find solutions while feeling anxious about events in my life. Walking down the hill on that morning after seeing the hawk, I stopped worrying. In that moment the value of 'floating' was profoundly obvious and the futility of worry was visibly apparent. The struggle to 'get somewhere' or to 'get ahead' can be exhausting when the path seems blocked! Sometimes one has to literally stop, inhale the breath of life and look around in order to see the way ahead. No amount of fretful thoughts can measure up to the richness of simply standing still and absorbing the timeless moment – because this enriches the core of our being where the marvel of guidance manifests and a direction forward becomes clear.

There was a time when I easily and perhaps innocently understood the rhythm and art of floating, which can be compared to a meditative state of being where one is receptively aware – without the grip of angst. To symbolically 'float', was for me, a cup of tea at an airport when I didn't know what my next step was, or floating in water when a silent place of timelessness was needed. That inherent consciousness to float seemed to have gone missing in recent years and on this day the hawk represented that timeless sensation that I had known before. This hawk, a manifestation and symbol of nature, reminded me of the insightful wisdom in recognizing a natural time for dynamic action and a time for restful silence.

A Lost Seagull

Pecking at crumbs on the hot tarmac road while dodging cars in the parking lot of this large supermarket, a young seagull seemed lost and far away from his natural habitat where the familiar waves of a salty cooling ocean would be home. I wanted to help him; he seemed vulnerable and hungry and yet persisted; he didn't give up trying to find food in a harsh and inhospitable setting.

When my sister sympathetically commented on the determination of this young gull, I was filled with admiration for such plucky perseverance. On this searing hot summer day, he must have been distressed and thirsty while trying to find food wherever he could. Shoppers were busy chatting and pushing their loaded shopping carts as they walked by the unassuming little bird.

Filled with innate compassion for the bird, a pang of sorrow at the plight of numerous humans who find themselves in a weak position also stirred me at that moment. Encountering harshly challenging circumstances, people are often passed by or ignored as they quietly struggle. It seems to be a popular inclination for fortunate members of society with ample resources to fill a shopping cart, to easily ignore others who valiantly struggle with survival.

We have eyes to see – do we really see? What an ironic world we live in where an underlying sense of self-absorbed desire will often blot out awareness for all but one's own immediate world of pleasure. Perhaps it is the grip of fear or trepidation of being in that same dreaded predicament oneself that generates an impulse to overlook those who are less comfortable.

A few months later while in Lyme Regis, I saw another young bird pushing an empty orange juice carton around, in the hope of finding some form of nourishment. Someone had tossed out their piece of litter onto this beautiful seaside rock and given the young seagull a fruitless sense of anticipation. The young gull persevered and continued the expectant effort to open this carton and find a tasty tidbit – to no avail. I decided to throw the carton away myself and liberate the bird so he could find some actual and natural food. Fish!

MEMORIES OF OUR DAD

Morning on the Estuary
Dad loved feeding the ducks and swans on the pier in Topsham; there was a special swan that always recognized him

"The present moment contains all time,
and within it, is all that can be hoped for, done and realized"

Kahlil Gibran

A Celebration of Dad's Life

Written by my brother, Dominic

It is a sad day, a sad time. We've lost our beloved father. A modest man. A shy man. A father and a grandfather. A man we loved and who loved us. An irreplaceable person.

We have all known him in a part of his life; for my siblings and I, as a father, for my nephews as a grandfather and for others he will have been a friend, a work colleague, a sailing partner or perhaps an acquaintance. For each of us he will have left a different yet distinct memory.

The death of my father, Julian, came suddenly and unexpectedly following a broken hip. A setback, which he stoically struggled to overcome.

To us his family, his death seems to herald the end of an era - losing our last parent and seemingly closing the door on that generation of our family. More broadly, his death seems to epitomize the demise of a national generation. Those men and women who valued honor and fair dealings, bringing those qualities to bear in the conduct of their everyday lives. A generation who gave their youth if not their lives during a World War. A generation from a bygone time.

My father was born in 1921 in Malaya. He was the youngest of four children, returning from Malaya at the age of three to attend boarding school in Cornwall. He later moved to Brussels with his mother before returning to England and settling in Portsmouth.

This is where he seemed most happy as a child and where his love of sailing was kindled. He was a great sportsman and spent every moment during the warmer months swimming, boating and cycling. As a family they spent many much loved summer holidays staying in St Helen's on the Isle of White. I remember his wonderful stories about their adventures during these pre-war family holidays. My father was immensely proud of his elder brothers, Bill and Harry. Bill, a suave Royal Naval Officer who played rugby and boxed for the Navy, and Harry who was a pilot in the early RAF before joining the merchant service and eventually emigrating to New Zealand. I grew up with stories about their boxing and rugby achievements.

During one family holiday on the Isle of White, while he watched his elder brothers playing cricket on the village green, War was declared, changing the lives of a generation in an instant.

My father immediately and proudly volunteered to join the Army only to be told he was too young and his time would come. His sense of duty was strong and through a family friend was directed to the Royal Navy. He served from that moment until the end of the War. His service included the dreaded North Atlantic convoys and the Eastern Med fleet. He was one of the crews to collect World War 1 US Navy vessels from Halifax, Nova Scotia and return with them to the UK, before taking them on to the Mediterranean. Later, he became a Royal Navy Commando leading landing parties in many operational theatres from the Eastern Med to the landings in Normandy. Throughout he maintained a respect for those around him both friend and foe. His sense of humanity has always been strong.

Towards the end of the War he met my mother, Elizabeth, or as he called her 'Blitz'. Following the war my father joined the Colonial Service and accepted a post in Uganda, East Africa. A country and role he enjoyed immensely. My family later returned to the UK, initially settling in Dorset and later in Topsham.

My father loved the countryside and being outside. He loved to go camping and I remember wonderful camping holidays in Cornwall and the Isle of Wight. I remember the meticulous preparation, the packing, the journeys and the putting up of tents. I remember on one occasion; I was a small boy and we were trying to find a particular campsite in Cornwall. I must have fallen asleep. During my slumber Dad had found some sweet scented Honeysuckle and when I awoke I found Dad had spread it around me and the air was full of the glorious scent.

It was in Topsham that he spent his retirement. He enjoyed sailing across to Dartmouth, sitting on his boat taking in the tranquility of the reed beds, striking conversation with other boat owners, simply spending his days on or around the river. He adored the simplicity the estuary offered.

I tell you these brief facts about my father, as I believe they have all contributed to his makeup, and ultimately to the makeup of my family. Understanding his life helps to make sense of our lives - our likes and dislikes. Our pre-dispositions. My father, like all of us, had his faults. Some of which he was aware and of some he was unaware. To me this is human and we rely upon those closest to us to help us to deal with these faults. To forgive us and to accept us as we are and for what we are. He also had great strengths. He had strong views of right and wrong, of fairness and of enjoying the world we are in.

Something my father was very clear about was that actions speak louder than words! For my father forgiveness was a process, a way of being in the world. My father was very much an advocate of decency, of treating people with respect, of understanding that we are all guilty of making mistakes and errors in judgment. He believed in moral courage and fortitude. He believed in duty and he believed in honor. He believed it is our actions that count and less so our words. He once said to me. "The road to hell is paved with good intentions. It's what you do that counts."

My father has given many things to his family, not material but a more important commodity. A sense of fair play, of decency, of respect, of standing up for what we believe in. Of not being afraid to be different or to think differently in a society where importance appears to be given over to profitability and efficiency. To my father 'business' was subject to good Government and not vice versa.

He grew up in a different world, a world where there had been privilege, where his family was lucky enough to have been privileged in the past. This world, for my father was also one of mutual respect and one where, as he repeatedly told me as child, "With privilege comes responsibility". The premise remained strong in his mind. For me, this simple but honorable sentiment sums up my Dad.

The unexpected nature of my father's death has given rise to many feelings for my family - bewilderment, surprise, the sense of being cheated out of something, plainly and simply put - pain and loss. The loss of a father and the pain of being denied the opportunity to say our goodbyes. I think some call this 'closure'. But my view is that we should not rush for this 'closure' or we will lose a wider perspective of the process we need to go through to achieve a true sense of acceptance.

To me the word 'closure' is simply too trite, it is borrowed from business language and should be reserved for business deals and real estate transactions. For me closure is not for the complex feelings we have toward the people we love. I have heard it better explained in the following way: "The loose threads, the unspoken sentences, the unintended wounds, the unfinished forgiveness, and the unrecoverable losses – we never 'get over' them. We never close the door on them, not entirely. They become part of us. We find a way to integrate all that sacred messiness into our new identities: to adapt and evolve, to learn to feel love and pain (often at the same time), and little by little to grow." For me this means we must learn to live without our Dad, to embrace what he stood for, what he brought to us and to take this forward adding it to our own legacies.

If I were asked to do the impossible and to sum up our Dad in a few thoughts I should have to say that his love for us has made us strong. That his sense of humor and mischievous smile lightened our lives. His moral courage inspired us and taught us compassion. Above all his selfless generosity to his family showed us what really matters.

Dad you gave your all to us your family, we were your greatest joy and I know each of us made you proud. We have been shaped by your sense of fair play and felt secure with the love you showed us.

Dad, we will miss that sparkle in your eye.

By Major Dominic Maxwell-Batten

Dad

Topsham Estuary, in Devon

Dominic, Thankyou!!

On November 8th, 2007 our family felt deeply unified as we saw and listened to our youngest sibling who stood facing the congregation in the church at Dad's funeral. With vulnerability and dignity he spoke directly from the heart. He spoke for us too while expressing the sadness that we each felt. Standing alone and courageous, Dominic touched us deeply. He stirred the whole church on that sad momentous day of our Dad's burial.

Dad, we miss you!

My brother, Dominic

Dad's Earlier Memories of Mum

After Mum died, my visits to England were filled with sunny outings in Topsham with Dad – he in his maroon red mobility buggy while I walked beside him on foot. Dad loved going to Mum's grave where we planted flowers and industriously weeded her small burial place, which was quite sacred to us. He said: "*we're going to see Mum*" as he sped off in his bright motorized transporter with me by his side. Once there, he raced off to the water tap so we could fill the cans and water Mum's flowers. Dad's face was content and happy as we planted bulbs and the colorful flora we had brought with us.

It was the summer of 2006 when her grave was a flowering mass of color; Dad and I felt pleased when people commented on the living flowering grave that we had artistically created. We felt a heartfelt pride to be sharing this visual joy with others. I sensed a pang of wistfulness in knowing that I would soon have to leave this flower garden and return to my home in USA, I wanted to tend the flowers and maintain this enchanting spot for others to feel consoled as they visited this place of rest. I knew that our time with dad was running out and it meant a great deal for me to honor this reality.

Dad and I often went to the Passage Pub. Sitting outside on the wooden benches and overlooking the pretty estuary, he enjoyed his sandwich and a cup of tea before pulling out his favorite binoculars to look out at the wildlife in the marshes. He always had his pipe and tobacco with him and it was on one of those occasions I asked him how he met Mum.

I knew that Mum had trained to be a nurse at Hasla Naval hospital where my parents met in 1944. Dad had just returned from Normandy and he used to sit alone in a boat to get some peace to unwind and to process the horrific aftermath of war. He pretended he was fishing so that people would not question this solitary figure. He only wanted to sit and bathe in the quiet evenings. By getting away from everything for a while he felt he could cope with the memories of a dreadful and brutal war.

One day a crowd of bubbly nurses turned up as he pulled his boat into shore. They chatted merrily together close by. As quickly as they appeared, they all left again - except for mum. That is when they met. From a distance, mum had seen dad on the boat many times before and wanted to meet this lone handsome young navy man. She had asked her friends to accompany her there, just for the friendly girlish encouragement.

A few months after my parents met, unknown to either of them, two of dad's aunts went to see mum's mother Florence Elvira, because they wanted to make sure that their nephew was mixing with the 'right' kind of person. I often heard my parents during their older years, with their amusing childlike quarrels, telling me that it was their family that wanted to inspect the other family! I still laugh now when I think of their childlike and comical squabbles in their elder years.

During the time when they met, dad's mother was in a vulnerable state and this in itself must have caused him a lot of concern; even though he was only twenty-three years old his mother had been placed in a nursing home while he was at war. His other siblings seemed uninterested and dad was understandably puzzled why they had abandoned their own mother after she had lost all her money. The memory was vague for him as I listened intently that afternoon; maybe he had partly blocked this weighty episode from his memory.

Mumsi-Di (dad's mum) must have been about fifty-four years old when he went to war, and fortunately his two Aunts took it upon themselves to be protective of dad's future prospects in marriage.

When mum moved to Portland Harbor, she was placed in charge of five hundred wrens and was responsible for their health care with only one medical doctor on call when needed. The Irish doctor who was theoretically in charge, left this young and dedicated naval nurse to run the sick bay; she was known as a hard worker and very efficient at her job. Thriving with the work, she adored that time in her life and gained a great deal of respect from people around her. She knew how to respond in emergency situations and her flourishing gift in caring for others was established and admired.

Mum used to walk up to the top of the hill from the shore in Weymouth to the wrens quarters at all hours of day and night and all kinds of weather conditions, to tend any sick wrens. Before becoming a nurse she joined the land army, which was organized by her mother; mum hated it and ran away in the middle of the night. Becoming a nurse fulfilled her in so many ways and she soon became an officer in the Navy. I always enjoyed the joyful expression in her face as she spoke about those days - she had a repertoire of numerous intriguing stories.

When mum used the Port Officers dinghy, she rowed herself out from Portland dock yard on her day off so she could catch crabs and supply the other wrens with a tasty meal of fresh seafood. The crabs would be lined up along the windowsills. Mum sank the Port Officer's dinghy one day because she tied it up when the tide was low, and when the tide came in, the boat sank. She couldn't understand where it had gone! When the port officer asked her where his boat was, she was mystified at the 'disappearance'. Then when the tide went out again there was the boat - flooded with water. Dad laughed fondly and his eyes were wide and soft as he related that story. Dad loved the way mum wore red ribbons in her pigtails, he said that it was cheery in such dismal times of war. This was one of Mum's qualities throughout her life; she would always try to find a joyful aspect when times were hard. Her own young life had been very harsh and filled with challenges; finding joy in simple things helped her to cope. I too learnt that from my mother.

Dad went on to relate that the American navy chaps, with more money to spend, would steal all the English girls and buy them presents. Not only that, they vandalized the trains by smashing windows and beating up seats. Dad said that the English chaps were often angry at the behavior of Americans and so they in turn played some pranks on the yanks!

I miss our Dad. He died suddenly on November 1st 2007 and my deep regret today is that I was not able to spend more time with him – I loved those outings as much as he did yet I was often compelled to work away from home during my visits to England and whenever I returned to Topsham especially during summer months dad and I went 'skipping' off on our outings. We went to the recreational field a few times where his boat TARKA (named after Tarka the Otter) was moored out in the estuary. Dad's face lit up as he gazed at Tarka through his binoculars and then he would tell me about the trips he made in her. He was quite an adventurous man well into his seventies and his boat provided him with hours of pleasure.

We went out some evenings to see the sunset over the estuary and one evening when it was the highest tide of the year, dad met a few of his friends who were thrilled to see him out and about, as they all chatted happily together. That evening, no sooner was Dad at home, with the excitement of a young boy he wanted to go out again!

There is now an empty void. I miss our parents' indelible personalities – most of all I miss their love and in writing about them I bathe in their presence for a little longer and hold on to them for just a little longer.

This is where Dad and I often had tea, while looking out at the boats.

This is dad's red boat, 'TARKA' (in the middle).

Boats moored on Topsham Quay

His Last Days

Dad died suddenly – just five weeks after an operation to repair a fractured hip.

With a loving and practical dedication, my two brothers Justin and Jonny took care of Dad at home for six years after Mum died. Finally in the summer of 2007, after falling and unable to get up, Dad needed twenty-four hour medical care and had to be transferred to an assessment center. He fell, broke his hip and was rushed to the hospital where he had a major operation to repair the hip. Jonny and I were there on that Sunday afternoon as Dad awoke from the anesthetic – he opened his eyes and smiled with a happy recognition when he saw us both. I was amazed that he came around from the anesthetic with such alertness after intense surgery. Sadly though, during the weeks that followed he wasn't recovering as we hoped; the nurses seemed too busy to help him eat and drink. I'd been visiting him in hospital and even though he was in a lot of pain and at a loss to know why his hip was hurting, he nevertheless always commented on the view: *"It looks like Malta,"* he said.

The ward was at the end of this large hospital in Exeter and his bed was next to a small window that overlooked some fields and even though the view was nothing spectacular, he was enjoying the fleeting recollection of a happy time in his life. He had found a chink of pleasure in a painful world. Each time we visited him, Dad never failed to tell us all that he loves us; I was finding a deep fulfillment in this bond with him. I'm warmed at the memories of his childlike and brightly welcoming eyes whenever he saw us.

We chose a cheery nursing home, which would be ready for him after the hospital. I was sure he would enjoy chatting with other residents and specially benefit from the various activities there. I was looking forward to having our Dad here with us for a bit longer.

The nurses were getting ready to discharge him when some strange and mysterious hospital bug kept preventing him from leaving the infected hospital. It was vague. It wasn't easy to get clear answers from the medical establishment, they seemed uncomfortable in an apparent attempt to conceal something which I can only conclude was the 'hospital bug' that was running rampant through hospitals in England.

I was due to leave for America and the nurses assured me that Dad was in no danger; they expected him to go to the nursing home as soon as the precautionary measures were lifted. They certainly gave me a misleading sense of assurance. Within ten days of my return to the USA - Dad died. According to a nurse, he had his lunch and an hour later died in his sleep. She flippantly informed me: “He’s at peace now”.
His death though abrupt and unexpected was plainly an outcome we foresaw yet we were all convinced he had a little more time left – even just a few months.

His sudden demise threw me into a grief stricken and distressed state. I’d been in England for four months and during that time as well as working, I’d been helping with Dad’s care – I was devastated that within ten days of my return to Texas, he died. I wasn’t with him during the time he died and I felt distraught. I couldn’t hold back from crying and sobbing.

Dad had a deeply compassionate side to him. He understood and even felt my anguish when as a young girl in my twenties, I lost my daughter. Whenever we spoke about it he winced with pain himself. I don’t know how I got through that time where I felt alone and abandoned - it was dad who truly heard and comforted me. Dad was the loving parent during those days, weeks and years when I re-lived the ache. Though mum was grief-stricken at the death of her granddaughter, her first reaction was to lash out and blame; she never really got over the loss and nor did I.

Dad had a difficult life. His childhood was lonely and fearful and teenage years were spent in shock while trying to console his mother when she lost her assets in the fall of the stock exchange. His youth was spent in a gruesome war and his adult years though sprinkled with happiness, were also filled with the worry of trying to support a growing family.

Co-incidentally one year before dad passed away, I had a beautiful dream about my grandmother Mumsi-Di; in the dream her immeasurable love emanated from her eyes and the very heart of her being, while embracing me with warmth. I had not dreamt about her before – she had died when I was only ten years old yet this dream had been so clear. I wondered at that moment whether she had come to tell me that dad's time in this world would soon be coming to an end.

One of the memories I will always hold close to my heart is the way Dad's face lit up when any of his children came to visit him in hospital – he loved us all and I was so glad that in his last days he knew that he had five devoted children.

Dad with Mumsi-Di in 1940.

Mumsi-Di, our grandmother lost her money in the crash of the stock exchange - dad joined the Navy and went to war.

Here he is on shore leave, with his beloved mother

Mum and Dad's Love

A month after dad died, I returned to England again so as to work as a caregiver and re-coup my bruised finances. The moment I boarded that airplane for the three-hour commute from San Antonio to Atlanta, it was as though I was pulled into another reality! At first this little plane appeared quite cozy and intimate, yet at the same time I couldn't believe how small it was.

During the whole trip I was immersed in a bubble of love, as though my parents were holding me in their arms. 'Floating' in a calm light of warmth, I sat back and allowed those feelings to embrace my body and soul because I knew that typically I would be terrified on such a narrow and almost claustrophobic aircraft. I knew that Mum and Dad were together and they were shielding me from a fear of flying. It was a gift, which I received with conscious gratitude and without question.

When the plane landed we stepped onto a stairway that had been wheeled up to the aircraft door; after walking carefully down these old fashioned moveable stairs and stepping onto the runway at the bottom with the other bemused passengers, we were directed through a makeshift hallway with a plastic covering. I felt that I was back in the 1950's when as a family we were traveling to and from Uganda. Landing at Entebbe airport and being met with one of those old style moveable set of steps, this present experience was uncannily linked to those past childhood memories of flying, as though for those three hours I had gone back in time. Then abracadabra, there I was walking through a doorway and into a huge modern airport - Atlanta! Everything had returned to the year 2007 again.

I knew then that mum and dad are together and their love is embracing us all the time. I can't possibly imagine anything else than that our parents are happy and their love surrounds all their children.

I was in for a hard time for the four following months in England, feeling alone and cut off. Mum and dad gave me a boosting gift for the solitary journey ahead.

They both had experienced a sad and lonely childhood; I'm so very glad that they were loved by five children in their older years and they both died with the warmth in knowing how much they were cherished.

“You look like a Fairy.....But.....

You’re As Clumsy As an Elephant!”

I can honestly laugh at those words now, even though during my teenage years it did have a confidence-bashing effect and indeed made me clumsier. Today I look back without any seeds of indignation; I don’t take it personally because I know that Dad loved his children. He was belittled while growing up and never having had the chance, time or even ability to process his own ‘shadows’, it popped out in the form of mocking and sarcastic remarks to his children. He tried hard to rise above it. Dad was devoted to his children and would never intentionally hurt any of us. His life had been particularly disappointing at that time; he felt that he had failed at a number of things – yet actually in reality he hadn’t failed. He had succeeded in the face of adversity to attain a degree in agriculture and land a successful job on the East African continent in the coffee industry. Loyalty to his family and the fact that we were all ill meant that we needed to return to England.

I can laugh at myself now – yes I can be clumsy and I can be very graceful too - especially when I'm dancing. I've been fortunate to have had opportunities in my life to travel, explore, discover – and look within myself. Dad didn't have those options. It's not always easy for someone to overcome his or her hurt and even frustration towards life. Dad tried his best.

I'm left now, after his death, with memories of his kindness. And this is my truth because I feel his immeasurable love.

Fairy elephant

Epilogue

In a television interview, a renowned author was asked why she writes: *"Because I love it and I need it"* She spoke about the redemptive strength of love: *"Love is the strongest power there is"*

Simple and honest – there is no other way for me to describe my own passion to write. Writing is my voice. Reading and writing can be an enchanting way to flee from reality for a short while and just as equally a way to be in touch with reality. There is a sense of community in our shared human journey when existent feelings and real situations are revealed and brought into the light of day – we're not alone in what we feel or long for.

After a law enforcement officer and a friend of mine spent the night of New Year working at the jail and being responsible for the running of the prison and inmates, he said to me: "*What a chaotic mass of suffering humanity – all chasing some desire for happiness*" He went on to quote the words of a well-known spiritual sage:

"There is nothing wrong with desire,

we just don't have enough of it –

we should desire complete union with the divine self".

****

At eighteen years old and with very little money, I spontaneously took off for a three-week hitchhiking adventure across Europe. It didn't take much persuasion from twenty-one year old Polly who was from America, to fire me up for this journey. She was working in England on a temporary working visa, at the *Valley of Rocks hotel* in Lynton North Devon; I was working as a hotel receptionist there for the summer months.

Polly was determined to see more of Europe while she had the chance, but didn't want to go alone. It was a trek that was completely unplanned from start to finish. We did have the sense to purchase a membership for youth hostels enabling us to sleep in protected and cheap lodgings, which also gave us the opportunity to meet other young travelers. Memories of eating fruit from some orchards in the French part of Switzerland or standing under an awning on the south coast of France when it was pouring with rain. Getting a delicious fresh fruit smoothie in an outside stall in Milan and sitting on the beach in Viareggio Italy, not knowing where we would sleep that night which didn't seem to fluster either of us. I suppose we were naïve to be so trusting and yet we were inexperienced, and we did innocently trust life! A friendly Italian couple who were selling melons on the beach saw us and with a maternal concern, took us in and fed us for two days. I do remember that time when we resolved to run away from a couple of suspicious looking men in France; after hiding under a bridge until they had gone, my heart was pounding with fear as well as the adrenalin of impending action.

Eating didn't seem a priority on that journey because I didn't feel hungry and the fact that I had no money left, predetermined that resolution. After three non-stop weeks of traveling, I lost one stone in weight and arrived back in England looking emaciated – yet happy.

On that unforgettable trip, while in Cannes I sat on the beach and looked out at the sunset, feeling overwhelmingly grateful to have stepped on continental soil. Fulfilled at completing this quest, I bought a postcard and sent it to my parents with the words: '*my day is done*'. At that point I was ready to make the journey back home to England. Satisfied that a profound voyage and a meaningful rite of passage had been attained, I felt worthy of self-respect.

Now after completing this book I find myself saying: '*my day is done*'. It is with gratitude, that I share words and feelings that flow and breathe through my heart and soul.

"Each of us is a book waiting to be written,
And if written, results in a person explained"

Thomas M. Cirignano

Let us not pray to be sheltered from dangers,

but to be fearless when facing them.

- Rabindranath Tagore

"Love exalts our
earthly bodies to heaven,
and makes the very hills
dance with joy"
RUMI
Shiva

A Poem By My Sister

Margherita Atkinson

Love shines on those
who show each other love.
Sun shines down on those,
with purity in their heart
Life is kind to those
who are true in heart and soul.
Love will only grow in people
when these things are kept true.
Two hearts' united,
create the birth of a new star in the sky

Ladram Bay

"In one atom are found all the elements of the earth;
In one motion of the mind are found the motions
of all the laws of existence.
In one drop of water are found the secrets
of all the endless oceans.
In one aspect of YOU
Are found all the aspects of existence"

Kahlil Gibran

Photo by Ritzy Ryciak

Charmiene Maxwell-Batten was born in Devon, England in the small town of Axminster. At six weeks old she left for Uganda, with her parents and brother Jonathan. Charmiene's father was a government inspector and consultant in the coffee industry on the East African continent.

Charmiene and her brother lived in Kampala for ten years as the family grew; those were joyful events when Justin and Margherita were born at Entebbe hospital in Kampala. Later when the family returned to England, Dominic our youngest sibling was born.

Charmiene has a profound interest in Natural health, alternative medicine, herbal remedies as well as an early and creative passion for ballet and writing, which has continued throughout her life.

Her many years in Switzerland, India, Thailand and USA have provided a deep appreciation for cultural diversity and her visits to three spiritual teachers in India have given her an understanding of our inner and human journey in this world. In 1992 she was inspired to write and share her experiences.

Charmiene's paternal great grandfather, Reverend Sabine Baring-Gould, the author of the well-known hymns 'Onward Christian Soldiers' and 'Now the Day is Over', was also an avid traveler and major literary figure, who was an authority on myths, legends and folklore. Baring-Gould was a friend and literary peer of George Bernard Shaw and Arthur Conan Doyle. His marriage to Grace Taylor was the basis of the character Eliza Doolittle in Pygmalion. Rumor has it that that his estate Lew Trenchard Manor in Dartmoor, provided the atmosphere and setting for Conan Doyle's 'Hound of the Baskervilles'. Baring Gould also appears as a character in Laurie King's Sherlock Holmes novel – 'The Moor'.

Sabine Baring-Gould

Charmiene at Lew Trenchard Manor 1993

Beautiful Dartmoor

"Do you see how every little breath of wind that sighed against the shore, was written down? The record of the weeping skies is brought to light; and now that which was hidden is revealed. He who has written these down on tables of stone, must have recorded the tears which fall on the earth and which to many, are unknown"

Sabine Baring-Gould

From his book 'The Mystery of Suffering'

I wonder whether my great grandfather felt lonely and often misunderstood – as I read his books written over a century ago, I’m profoundly touched by the insight and awareness. I even wonder if today he is fully appreciated for all his written work. Besides the acclaim for having written the hymn ‘Onward Christian Soldiers’ – his capacity for depth and understanding should stir the consciousness and soul of any spiritual seeker today.

Charmiene Maxwell-Batten

'Intuitive author Charmiene Maxwell-Batten offers readers a model for finding the depth of life in this sweet collection of contemplative writings. Elegant but informal, the author's tone invites friendly participation in her musings. For readers' interested finding a delicious loveliness in the everyday as well as those willing to be touched and changed by life's most striking challenges, this book is a blessing. '

Ceci Miller

www.ingramcontent.com/pod-product-compliance
Ingram Content Group UK Ltd.
Pitfield, Milton Keynes, MK11 3LW, UK
UKHW041945190726
13854UKWH00004B/1796